Baby Boomers

Acid Rock to Acid Reflux

Written by
Aaron Freeman
Rebecca Rock

new seasons®

Sonny and Cher they weren't, but no one had the heart to tell them.

8

"This is ridiculous. I didn't even shave my legs in the '60s!"

To people having acid flashbacks, this black-and-white photo may appear to be in color.

12

"My kids call this my Afro-Alien phase."

The only chicks following Charlie around now are from his chicken coop.

14

American Boomer Gothic

With a nip, a tuck, and a lot of electrolysis, Robert's transformation was complete.

19

He might have lost the golf match, but James was determined to win the race to the dining room for the early bird special.

"Okay, who stole my reading glasses?"

23

Acid rock to acid reflux

Yearbook photos don't always stand the test of time.

27

Literally the highest note
Larry had ever played.

Everyone recognized Ron at the 35-year class reunion. He hadn't changed a bit.

31

Although Sally always said she would roller-skate 'til she dropped, nobody actually *believed* her.

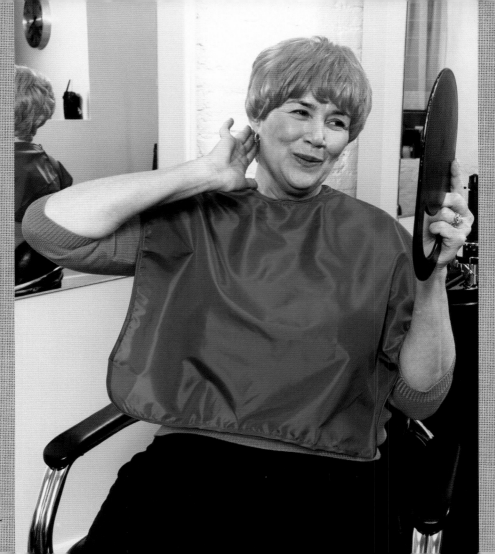

Frenchie turns 50.

It wasn't his trusty old street rod, but when Bob played with his toy cars, he could almost smell the burning rubber.

"*S*ag! You're it!"

Ever since Slasher's mom sent him that etiquette book...

41

Reverend Johnson parked the church bus in The Haight for 15 minutes, and this is what he came back to.

Nancy was convinced this ritual would take her on that magic carpet ride she'd dreamed of.

Militants in their college days, Sara and Ed still fought over every little thing.

Debbie passed through the five stages of grief: anger, denial, bargaining, ice cream, and, finally, acceptance.

Grant's brother told him this shirt would make him a chick magnet.

The shocking thing is, many in the crowd believed Roy and Roger really *were* holding up the sky.

From "I love you, Ringo!"
to "I've got Bingo!"

Power to the prostate!

"**I**f you must know, it's liquid Viagra®."

The love child of Lucille Ball and Don King.

From fab to flab.

It wasn't her old man's hog, but it got her around the retirement village just fine.

Mod Squad wannabes.

"She laughs at me,
she laughs at me not."

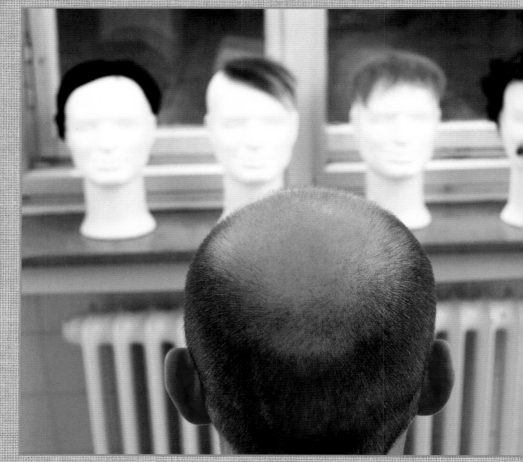

1966: Long hair
2006: Longing for hair

"When everyone else was listening to the Stones, I stuck with The King."

"People used to tell me
I look a lot like Grace Slick."

Then: The best of friends.

Now: A happily married couple.